Backyard Rabbits Farming Made Easy: From Novice to Expert

The Ultimate Step-by-Step Practical Guide to High-Yield Meat and Maximum Profit

Charles James

Table of Contents

Chapter 1: Introduction to Backyard Rabbit Farming
1.1 Why Raise Rabbits?
1.2 Choosing the Right Breeds for Meat and Profit
1.3 Setting Goals for Yield and Profitability

Chapter 2: Setting Up Your Rabbitry
2.1 Space and Housing Requirements
2.2 Choosing or Building the Ideal Hutch
2.3 Essential Equipment and Supplies

Chapter 3: Feeding and Nutrition for Optimal Growth
3.1 Basics of Rabbit Nutrition
3.2 Feed Types: Commercial vs. Natural Feed
3.3 Creating a Feeding Schedule

Chapter 4: Breeding for Maximum Meat Production

4.1 Selecting Breeding Pairs
4.2 Managing Breeding Cycles
4.3 Caring for Pregnant Does and Newborn Kits

Chapter 5: Health and Wellness in Your Rabbitry

5.1 Common Diseases and Their Prevention
5.2 Vaccinations and Veterinary Care
5.3 Daily Care Practices to Ensure Health

Chapter 6: Harvesting and Processing for Meat Yield

6.1 When and How to Harvest for Best Yield
6.2 Humane Slaughter and Processing
6.3 Meat Storage and Handling Tips

Chapter 7: Maximizing Profit in Rabbit Farming

7.1 Selling Rabbit Meat: Markets and Pricing
7.2 Additional Revenue Streams (Pelts, Manure, etc.)

7.3 Building a Customer Base and Marketing Your Rabbits

Chapter 8: Scaling Up Your Rabbitry for Higher Yield
8.1 Expanding Housing and Herd Size
8.3 Cost Analysis for Scaling Profitably

Chapter 9: Troubleshooting Common Challenges
9.1 Addressing Poor Growth and Low Yield
9.2 Managing Stress and Behavioral Issues
9.3 Preventing Losses and Maximizing Efficiency

Chapter 10: Building a Sustainable, Profitable Rabbit Farming Operation

Chapter 1

Introduction to Backyard Rabbit Farming

1.1 Why Raise Rabbits?

Raising rabbits in your backyard might sound unusual, but for many, it's one of the most rewarding and efficient ways to produce fresh, sustainable meat right at home. Rabbit farming has been practiced for generations, thanks to the animal's adaptability, low-maintenance requirements, and excellent return on investment. Whether you're new to backyard farming or simply exploring alternative ways to make the most of your outdoor space, raising rabbits could be a valuable, fulfilling venture.

1. High-Quality, Healthy Meat Production

Rabbits provide a lean source of protein that's low in fat and high in nutrients. Their meat is known to be tender and flavorful, often compared to chicken but with even less fat. This makes rabbit meat a healthier option, ideal for those looking to maintain a balanced diet. Moreover, by raising rabbits yourself, you have full control over their diet and living conditions, ensuring a clean and healthy meat source without unnecessary additives or antibiotics.

2. Efficient Use of Space and Resources

Rabbits are small animals, so they don't require large enclosures. Unlike larger livestock, rabbits can thrive in a modestly sized backyard setup. A few square feet per rabbit is generally sufficient, making them ideal for those with limited space. They also eat relatively small amounts of food, primarily hay, leafy greens, and pellets, which are affordable and easy to manage. This efficiency in space and food use translates to a lower environmental footprint and manageable costs for the farmer.

3. Quick Reproduction Rate for Sustainable Yield

Rabbits are known for their rapid reproductive cycle, which can be advantageous for a small-scale farmer. A pair of healthy rabbits can produce several litters a year, with each litter often containing five to twelve kits (baby rabbits). This high reproductive rate allows for a sustainable supply of meat throughout the year, enabling you to harvest regularly without depleting your stock.

4. Easy to Care For

Rabbits are relatively low-maintenance animals, especially compared to other livestock. They require clean water, proper food, and regular but simple cleaning of their enclosures. Additionally, they are naturally clean animals and rarely suffer from common diseases, making them less vulnerable to health issues if properly cared for. As a result, even beginners can raise rabbits successfully with minimal experience.

5. Beneficial for Your Garden

Rabbit droppings are an excellent fertilizer, rich in nitrogen and phosphorus, which makes them ideal for vegetable gardens and flower beds. Unlike some other animal waste, rabbit manure can be applied directly to the soil without needing to be composted first, saving time and making it a convenient, natural way to enrich your garden soil. By raising rabbits, you not only gain fresh meat but also a steady supply of organic fertilizer that helps your plants thrive.

6. Educational and Fulfilling Experience

Raising rabbits can be a meaningful activity for families, teaching children about responsibility, animal care, and the importance of sustainable practices. For adults, it's an opportunity to learn about animal husbandry and deepen their connection to the food they consume. Many backyard farmers find joy in the process, discovering that raising rabbits offers both practical benefits and emotional fulfillment.

Backyard rabbit farming is an accessible, sustainable way to produce high-quality meat, improve garden soil, and enjoy the process of raising animals. With modest space, minimal resources, and a little dedication, you can raise rabbits that not only contribute to your family's food supply but also enrich your gardening efforts. For anyone interested in self-sufficiency, healthy eating, and practical farming, raising rabbits in the backyard is a rewarding and realistic step toward a more sustainable lifestyle.

1.2 Choosing the Right Breeds for Meat and Profit

Backyard rabbit farming has become a popular choice for those interested in raising small livestock for both meat and income. Rabbits are efficient animals that require minimal space and resources yet yield a significant return in terms of meat production and potential profit. One of the most important decisions to make when starting a backyard rabbit farm is choosing the right breeds. Different rabbit breeds have unique qualities, and selecting the best breed can make a substantial difference in your farm's success.

Why Breed Selection Matters

Each rabbit breed has specific characteristics that affect growth rate, meat quality, and reproductive potential. For anyone aiming to maximize meat yield and profit, it's essential to choose a breed that aligns with these goals. Some breeds are naturally larger, grow faster, and have a higher meat-to-bone ratio, while others might be smaller and better suited for different purposes, such as fur production or companionship.

Key Factors to Consider in Choosing a Breed

1. Growth Rate: Faster-growing breeds will reach market weight sooner, allowing you to cycle through more litters and potentially earn a steady income. Fast-growing breeds are also cost-effective since they consume fewer resources over their lifespan.

2. Size and Meat Quality: Larger breeds typically produce more meat, making them ideal for farmers focused on meat production. Additionally, the texture and flavor of the meat can vary by breed, so it's wise to select breeds known for good meat quality if your goal is to sell or consume the meat.

3. Reproductive Efficiency: Breeds that are prolific breeders can increase profitability, as they allow for more frequent breeding cycles and larger litters. This means more rabbits for meat production and sale.

4. Adaptability and Hardiness: Rabbits that adapt well to your local climate and backyard environment are easier to manage and less prone to health issues. Choosing a hardy breed minimizes risks and reduces the need for medical intervention.

Popular Meat Breeds for Backyard Rabbit Farming

1. New Zealand: Known for its excellent meat-to-bone ratio, rapid growth, and calm temperament, the New Zealand rabbit is one of the most popular choices for meat production. They reach market weight quickly and are also known for their high fertility rates.

2. Californian: Another favorite for meat, the Californian rabbit is known for its hardiness and efficient feed-to-meat conversion rate. They have a muscular build and produce tender meat, making them ideal for backyard farmers.

3. Flemish Giant: As one of the largest rabbit breeds, the Flemish Giant offers a substantial meat yield. However, they require more space and food, so they may be more challenging to raise in a smaller backyard setup.

4. Champagne d'Argent: This French breed is recognized for its quality meat and attractive silver fur. While not as large as the Flemish

Giant, it provides a good balance of size, growth rate, and adaptability.

5. Satin: Satins are medium-sized rabbits that produce tender, flavorful meat. They are efficient breeders and easy to manage, making them a suitable option for both beginners and experienced farmers.

Selecting the right breed for backyard rabbit farming is a critical step in ensuring the success of your venture. By focusing on breeds that meet your goals for meat production, growth rate, and adaptability, you lay a strong foundation for a profitable and sustainable rabbit farming operation.

1.3 Setting Goals for Yield and Profitability

Backyard rabbit farming can be a rewarding venture for both personal consumption and potential profit. However, like any agricultural project, success hinges on setting clear, achievable goals right from the start. This introductory guide provides a foundation for those new to backyard rabbit farming who want to raise rabbits effectively for meat yield and profit.

1. Understanding Your Purpose

Before you even set up a hutch, it's essential to clarify why you're raising rabbits. Are you primarily interested in supplying meat for your family, reducing food costs, or creating a secondary income source? Knowing this will guide every decision, from choosing rabbit breeds to designing your setup.

For Family Meat Supply: If you aim to provide a healthy, sustainable meat source for your household, you may only need a few breeding pairs.

For Profit: If profitability is the main goal, you'll need to plan for higher productivity, focusing on breeds, feeding efficiency, and marketing to potential buyers.

2. Choosing Breeds for Yield and Profit

Different rabbit breeds vary in size, growth rates, and meat quality, so selecting the right breed is key to reaching your goals. For example, New Zealand Whites, Californians, and Flemish Giants are popular for meat production due to their larger size and rapid growth rates. Investing time in research and possibly consulting with experienced rabbit farmers will help you choose a breed that aligns with your objectives.

3. Setting Production Goals

Establishing production goals is essential for keeping your operation on track. Begin by deciding how much meat or income you aim to produce each month or year. For example, if you wish to generate 20 pounds of meat per month, you'll need to determine how many rabbits you should raise and breed to meet that target.

4. Planning for Cost Efficiency

Profitability in rabbit farming depends heavily on managing costs effectively. Take time to budget for expenses, **including:**

Housing: Sturdy hutches, fencing, and maintenance costs.

Feed: Rabbits need a balanced diet, which can include pellets, hay, and garden vegetables. Growing some of their food can reduce costs.

Health and Maintenance: Budget for preventive care, any needed medications, and general upkeep.

Tracking costs helps ensure that your income (if selling) or savings (if consuming) outweighs your expenses.

5. Building a Sales Strategy (if selling)

If you plan to sell rabbit meat, fur, or by-products, establish a sales strategy early. Decide where you will sell your rabbits and who your customers will be. This could involve local farmers' markets, community members, or even local restaurants looking for quality meat. Remember to check local regulations on selling rabbit products.

6. Monitoring and Adjusting Goals

Finally, like any successful project, backyard rabbit farming requires continuous evaluation. Track your production, sales, and costs each month to see how you're progressing toward your goals. Adjust as needed – sometimes slight changes to feed, breeding cycles, or selling strategies can make a significant difference.

By setting clear goals, monitoring your progress, and being willing to adapt, you can make backyard rabbit farming a sustainable source of food, income, or both.

Chapter 2

Setting Up Your Rabbitry

2.1 Space and Housing Requirements

Creating the right space for your rabbits is one of the most critical steps to successful backyard rabbit farming. Not only does proper housing ensure your rabbits are healthy and comfortable, but it also impacts productivity and growth. Here's a breakdown of the essentials for setting up a safe, practical, and efficient rabbitry in your backyard.

1. Choosing the Right Location

Protection from Elements: Rabbits are sensitive to extreme weather conditions. Place your rabbitry in a shaded area that provides relief from direct sun in summer and shelter from wind and rain in colder months. A barn, shed, or lean-to can offer some protection.

Good Drainage: Choose a location with good drainage. This prevents water pooling, which can lead to muddy, damp conditions—breeding grounds for diseases. Slightly elevated areas work best for keeping things dry.

Accessibility: Place the rabbitry close to your home for ease of access. This makes feeding, cleaning, and monitoring much simpler, especially during bad weather.

2. Understanding Space Needs

Cage Size: Each rabbit should have enough space to stand up on its hind legs, stretch out, and move around comfortably. A general rule is to allow at least 3 to 4 square feet per rabbit for adults. Larger breeds need more space.

Multi-Level Setup: If you're raising many rabbits but have limited backyard space, consider a multi-level cage structure. Each level should be sturdy, with secure flooring and proper ventilation.

Exercise Space: While rabbits can stay healthy in cages, they also benefit from exercise outside of their enclosures. If you have the space, set up a secure, fenced exercise area where they can run and play. This prevents boredom and supports overall health.

3. Choosing Housing Types

Hutches or Cages: Rabbit hutches or cages are the most common types of rabbit housing. Hutches are often made of wood with wire floors, which allow waste to fall through. Be sure to use a comfortable resting area, like a piece of wood or plastic mat, to protect rabbits' feet from the wire.

Pens and Runs: For those with more space, outdoor pens or runs provide a more natural environment. Make sure the fencing is secure, with fine mesh to keep out predators and prevent rabbits from escaping.

Nesting Boxes: If you plan to breed your rabbits, nesting boxes are essential for does (female rabbits) to give birth and care for their young. These boxes should be warm, dry, and private.

4. Ventilation and Lighting

Air Circulation: Good airflow is essential to prevent the buildup of ammonia from urine, which can be harmful to rabbits. If the rabbitry is indoors or partially enclosed, ensure it's well-ventilated. Fans can help in warm months.

Natural Light: Rabbits need a balance of light and dark to stay healthy. If they're kept indoors, make sure they receive some natural sunlight during the day but have a shaded area to retreat. Avoid direct sunlight in the summer, as rabbits overheat easily.

5. Sanitation and Waste Management

Cleanable Surfaces: Choose materials for cages and hutches that are easy to clean, such as wire and plastic. Wood can harbor bacteria, so it should be used sparingly or with waterproof coatings.

Regular Cleaning: Maintain a strict cleaning routine to control odors and prevent disease. Remove waste, clean feeders and waterers, and sanitize cages at least once a week.

Composting Rabbit Waste: Rabbit manure is highly valued as a fertilizer, as it's rich in nutrients and doesn't need to be composted before use. Set up a composting area near the rabbitry to make use of this resource.

6. Protecting from Predators

Secure Fencing: Rabbits are vulnerable to predators like dogs, raccoons, and birds of prey. Use strong, fine-mesh wire fencing around your rabbitry, ideally buried a few inches into the ground to prevent animals from digging under.

Covered Runs: If your rabbits are kept in outdoor runs, cover them to protect against hawks or other flying predators.

Locking Mechanisms: Use locks or latches on cages and hutches. Some animals, such as raccoons, are adept at opening simple latches.

By carefully setting up your rabbitry to meet these space and housing requirements, you'll create an environment where your rabbits can thrive. Thoughtful planning and routine maintenance will ensure their well-being, leading to healthier, more productive rabbits and a smoother, more enjoyable farming experience.

2.2 Choosing or Building the Ideal Hutch

A well-designed rabbit hutch is essential to a successful backyard rabbit farming setup. Whether you decide to buy a ready-made hutch or build one yourself, it's important to ensure it meets your rabbits' needs and supports the goals of your rabbitry. **Here's a step-by-step guide to**

choosing or building a hutch that will help your rabbits thrive while making your work easier.

1. Understanding the Basics: Rabbit Comfort and Health

Rabbits are social, curious animals that require a safe, comfortable, and clean living space. The ideal hutch provides protection from predators and extreme weather, adequate space for exercise, and an easy-to-clean environment that keeps them healthy. When considering a hutch design or selection, think about:

Space: Each rabbit needs room to hop, stretch, and stand on its hind legs comfortably. Plan for a minimum of 8 square feet per rabbit, though larger breeds and breeding does may need more.

Ventilation: Good airflow is crucial to prevent respiratory issues, so ensure there are ventilation openings in the hutch. This is particularly important if you're housing multiple rabbits in close proximity.

Protection from Elements: Your hutch should shield rabbits from rain, direct sunlight, and strong winds. A solid roof and enclosed sides can help achieve this, with enough ventilation to maintain fresh air.

2. Choosing the Right Location for Your Hutch

Placing your hutch in the right location in your backyard is just as important as its design. **Look for a spot that offers:**

Shade and Shelter: Rabbits don't tolerate extreme heat well, so keep the hutch in a shaded area or one that receives only morning sunlight.

Elevated Ground: Positioning the hutch on higher ground prevents flooding and helps keep the hutch dry, especially in rainy conditions.

Access to Clean Food and Water: Ensure there is an easy way to refill water bowls and provide fresh hay and food regularly.

When it comes to design, you can opt for either a stationary or mobile hutch, depending on your needs and space:

Stationary Hutches: Typically larger and built with solid frames, stationary hutches are ideal if you plan to house a few rabbits permanently in one location. Ensure these have raised floors, allowing droppings to fall through and improving cleanliness.

Mobile Hutches or Tractors: For those looking to rotate their rabbits around the yard, a mobile hutch (often called a rabbit tractor) lets rabbits forage safely on fresh grass. Make sure it's light enough to move but secure enough to protect rabbits from predators.

If you're building your own hutch, consider using materials that are safe for rabbits. Avoid treated wood or any materials that could be toxic if chewed. Plywood, untreated pine, and wire mesh (for parts like floors and sides) are commonly used in homemade hutches.

4. Keeping Your Hutch Clean and Functional

A clean hutch promotes good health and makes management easier. Choose a design with removable trays or wire floors that allow droppings to fall through, simplifying cleanup. A drop pan underneath is another useful feature for easy waste collection.

Rabbits benefit from fresh bedding, such as straw or wood shavings, changed regularly to prevent odors and health issues. If possible, elevate the hutch slightly off the ground to improve ventilation, reduce moisture buildup, and make it easier to clean underneath.

5. Adding Important Features

Once the basics are in place, consider adding features to enhance your hutch's comfort and efficiency:

Nest Boxes: For breeding does, nest boxes are essential for the safety of newborn kits. Make sure they are secure and easy to access for cleaning.

Water and Feeding System: Automatic watering systems or hanging water bottles can save time and help keep water clean. A hay feeder or rack will help keep food off the hutch floor, minimizing waste and promoting hygiene.

Weatherproofing: If you live in an area with harsh winters, consider adding insulation to the hutch or creating a wind block with plywood. For hot climates, cooling elements like a frozen water bottle placed inside the hutch can help rabbits beat the heat.

6. Long-Term Maintenance and Upgrades

As you expand your rabbitry or your needs evolve, you might want to upgrade the hutch. Whether you're adding more space, reinforcing materials, or installing new feeders, always prioritize rabbit comfort, health, and safety. Regular maintenance—like checking for wear in the wire, repairing damaged wood, and ensuring secure latches—is key to a long-lasting hutch.

The ideal rabbit hutch offers a safe, spacious, and clean environment for your rabbits, making backyard rabbit farming easier and more rewarding. By investing time in choosing or building a hutch that meets these standards, you set a strong foundation for a healthy, productive rabbitry.

2.3 Essential Equipment and Supplies

Setting up a rabbitry in your backyard is a rewarding way to produce fresh, healthy meat while managing your space effectively. For a smooth and successful operation, having the right equipment and supplies is crucial. **Here's a guide to help you set up an efficient, humane, and well-organized rabbitry.**

1. Rabbit Housing

Cages or Hutches: Your rabbits need spacious, secure, and well-ventilated housing. Most backyard setups use wire cages or wooden hutches. Cages with wire flooring allow waste to drop through, making cleaning easier. If you choose wooden hutches, ensure proper ventilation and regular cleaning to prevent moisture and odor buildup.

Pens and Runs: If you have extra space, consider outdoor runs where rabbits can exercise and graze. Make sure these areas are predator-proof and offer shade to protect from overheating.

2. Feeding Supplies

Feeders: Gravity feeders are ideal for ensuring your rabbits always have access to fresh pellets. These feeders are easy to refill and help reduce spillage, saving on feed costs.

Hay Racks: High-quality hay is a staple in a rabbit's diet. Hay racks keep the hay off the ground, reducing waste and contamination.

Water Bottles or Bowls: Rabbits need a constant supply of clean water. Automatic water systems with nozzles are convenient, or you can use large-capacity water bottles and bowls that are easy to refill.

3. Cleaning and Maintenance Tools

Scrapers and Brushes: These tools make cleaning cages, floors, and other surfaces quick and effective, keeping your rabbitry hygienic.

Disinfectant: Use a rabbit-safe disinfectant regularly to sanitize cages and feeding areas. This helps prevent disease spread and keeps your rabbits healthy.

Waste Disposal System: Rabbit droppings are excellent fertilizer for gardens. Collect waste efficiently with trays or bins that can be easily emptied, allowing you to repurpose it for your garden or sell it as natural fertilizer.

4. Breeding and Nesting Supplies

Nest Boxes: If you plan to breed rabbits, nest boxes are essential. These boxes should be placed in the cage about a week before the doe is due. Line them with hay or straw for comfort and warmth.

Identification Tools: For a larger operation, consider tagging or marking rabbits to track breeding history, health, and lineage.

Weighing Scale: Regular weighing helps you monitor the health and growth of kits and adults, especially in a breeding setup.

5. Safety and Shelter

Shade and Weather Protection: Protect rabbits from extreme weather with covers or shade structures. Rabbits can overheat easily, so ensure they have cool areas in the summer and are shielded from rain and cold winds in winter.

Predator Protection: Secure your rabbitry with fencing to keep predators out. Be sure that cages are elevated or protected on all sides to prevent access from animals like raccoons, dogs, or hawks.

6. Record Keeping

Log Book: A simple notebook or spreadsheet can track feeding, breeding, health checks, and production. Maintaining records helps you optimize your setup over time and make informed breeding and feeding decisions.

7. Emergency Kit

Basic First Aid: Keep a small first-aid kit with essentials like antiseptic, bandages, and styptic powder for minor injuries.

Medication: Have some common medications on hand for emergencies. Consult a vet about what to include, as certain ailments like infections may need immediate attention.

Thermometer: Knowing how to check temperatures can help monitor for illness or temperature extremes.

Setting up your rabbitry with the right equipment and supplies ensures a smooth operation that is both productive and humane. A well-equipped rabbitry not only supports the rabbits' health and welfare but also makes your management easier and more enjoyable. As you build out your rabbitry, start with the essentials and expand as needed based on your experience and goals.

Chapter 3

Feeding and Nutrition for Optimal Growth

3.1 Basics of Rabbit Nutrition

In backyard rabbit farming, understanding the basics of rabbit nutrition is essential to raise healthy, fast-growing rabbits that will meet your goals for meat and profit yield. **Here's a simple guide to feeding your rabbits right for steady, balanced growth.**

1. The Core Diet: Hay as a Staple

Hay is the foundation of a rabbit's diet. Fresh, high-quality hay is essential for their digestion, and it keeps their teeth naturally worn down. Grass hays like Timothy, orchard grass, or meadow hay are ideal. Avoid alfalfa hay for adult rabbits, as it's too high in protein and calcium, which can lead to health issues. However, young growing rabbits benefit from the extra protein and nutrients in alfalfa.

Tip: Ensure hay is available at all times to support continuous chewing and to prevent digestive issues.

2. Pellets: A Nutrient Boost

Commercial rabbit pellets are concentrated, nutrient-rich food designed to supplement hay and provide essential vitamins and minerals. Look for high-quality pellets with a protein content of about 14-16% for adults, though younger rabbits may need higher levels. Be cautious not to overfeed pellets, as they are calorie-dense and can lead to obesity if given in excess.

Tip: Measure pellet portions based on your rabbit's age, weight, and activity level to avoid overfeeding.

3. Fresh Vegetables and Greens: Variety and Fiber

Adding fresh vegetables and leafy greens to your rabbit's diet provides natural fiber, hydration, and extra vitamins. Choose leafy greens like romaine lettuce, parsley, or cilantro, and avoid high-oxalate greens like spinach and kale in large amounts. Introduce new veggies slowly to avoid upsetting their sensitive digestive systems.

Tip: Feed greens in small portions, especially when introducing new types, to help them adjust and monitor any digestive changes.

4. Water: Fresh and Clean Always

Rabbits need a steady supply of clean, fresh water to stay hydrated. Water is critical for their digestive health and for preventing heat stress. Use a clean water bottle or a heavy dish that can't be tipped over, and check it daily to ensure it's full and free from debris.

Tip: In hot weather, check their water more frequently, as rabbits are susceptible to heat and may need more hydration.

5. Avoiding Harmful Foods

Not all foods are safe for rabbits. Avoid sugary or starchy foods like fruits (in large amounts), bread, or any processed human food. These can disrupt their digestion and lead to serious health issues.

Tip: Treats like carrots or fruits should be given sparingly as occasional rewards, not daily staples.

6. Feeding Routine and Consistency

Rabbits are creatures of habit and do best with a regular feeding routine. Aim to feed them at the same time each day, with a balance of hay, pellets, and fresh greens. This consistency helps prevent overeating and reduces stress, leading to more content and healthy rabbits.

Tip: Watch their eating habits daily, as sudden changes can be an early sign of illness.

Proper rabbit nutrition is straightforward but must be carefully managed. With a diet based on high-quality hay, measured pellets, fresh greens, and clean water, your backyard rabbits can thrive and grow steadily. Healthy nutrition not only improves growth rates but also enhances their overall quality of life, benefiting both your rabbits and your farm's productivity.

3.2 Feed Types: Commercial vs. Natural Feed
Feeding is one of the most important aspects of raising healthy, productive rabbits in backyard farming. Understanding the differences between commercial and natural feeds can help you make the best choices for optimal growth and yield. **Let's break down what each feed type offers and what you should consider.**

1. Commercial Feed: A Convenient, Balanced Option

Commercial rabbit feed is specially formulated to provide balanced nutrition in every bite.

Typically available as pellets, these feeds are designed by nutritionists to support healthy growth, reproduction, and fur quality.

Advantages of Commercial Feed:

Complete Nutrition: Commercial feeds usually contain a balanced mix of proteins, carbohydrates, fiber, vitamins, and minerals. This takes the guesswork out of feeding, as everything your rabbit needs is in one product.

Convenience: Pellets are easy to store, measure, and feed. They're ideal if you want a straightforward feeding routine.

Consistent Growth: With commercial feed, you can expect predictable growth and weight gain, which can be important if you're raising rabbits for meat or breeding purposes.

Drawbacks of Commercial Feed:

Cost: Commercial feed can be more expensive than natural or homemade options, especially if you're raising many rabbits.

Dependency: If you rely solely on commercial feed, your rabbits could become less resilient to changes in diet. Also, if your supplier runs out or prices increase, it could impact your feeding strategy.

Processed Ingredients: Some commercial feeds contain additives, preservatives, or fillers. For those who prefer a more natural approach, this can be a concern.

2. Natural Feed: Fresh, Cost-Effective, and Locally Sourced

Natural feed includes fresh greens, hay, vegetables, and grains that you can grow or gather yourself. It's a more hands-on approach that allows for flexibility and creativity in feeding.

Advantages of Natural Feed:

Cost Savings: Sourcing greens, garden waste, and natural grains can be much cheaper than buying commercial pellets, especially if you're able to grow or forage a significant amount.

Nutritional Variety: Natural feed offers a wide range of nutrients from different plants. This variety can promote resilience in your rabbits by helping them adapt to seasonal changes in diet.

Health Benefits: Fresh greens and natural foods are packed with fiber, which promotes healthy digestion, and antioxidants, which support immunity. Feeding rabbits fresh, nutrient-rich plants can result in a higher quality of meat and fur.

Drawbacks of Natural Feed:

Labor-Intensive: Collecting, preparing, and ensuring variety in natural feed requires time and effort. You'll need to educate yourself on which v4plants are safe and nutritious and ensure they're free of pesticides.

Nutritional Balance: Ensuring balanced nutrition can be challenging. Rabbits need a diet high in fiber but controlled in protein and fat to prevent obesity and digestive issues.

Seasonal Availability: Depending on your location, some plants may not be available year-round, requiring planning and perhaps a mix of natural and commercial feed.

3. Best Practices for Optimal Growth

To support the healthy growth of your backyard rabbits, **here are some feeding tips:**

Combine Both Types: A hybrid approach, mixing commercial pellets with natural forage, can offer balance and flexibility. This gives your rabbits access to the consistency of commercial feed while benefiting from the variety of fresh foods.

Focus on Hay: Hay, especially timothy or meadow hay, should be the staple of any rabbit's diet. It supports digestion and provides essential fiber, helping avoid common health issues.

Introduce New Foods Gradually: Rabbits have sensitive digestive systems, so always introduce new foods slowly to avoid stomach upset.

Supplement with Vegetables and Herbs: Fresh, pesticide-free vegetables like carrots (in moderation), leafy greens, and herbs (like parsley or basil) make excellent supplements and enrich your rabbits' diet.

In backyard rabbit farming, both commercial and natural feeds have their places. Commercial feed offers ease and consistency, while natural feed provides variety and a closer-to-nature approach. Many rabbit farmers find a mix of the two best supports their goals, allowing for balanced nutrition while keeping costs manageable. By combining these options, you can raise healthy rabbits that grow well, produce high-quality meat and fur, and enjoy a balanced, nutritious diet.

3.3 Creating a Feeding Schedule

Creating a feeding schedule for backyard rabbits is essential to ensure their growth, health, and productivity. With a structured approach to feeding, you can maximize both the meat yield and overall health of your rabbits, making the most of your efforts in raising them. **Let's break down what an effective feeding schedule looks like, focusing on balanced nutrition, consistent timing, and the benefits of natural foods.**

1. Understand Rabbit Nutritional Needs

Fiber is Key: Rabbits have a digestive system that thrives on high-fiber foods. Fiber helps keep their gut healthy and aids in digestion. The best source of fiber is quality hay, such as timothy or meadow hay, which should make up around 70% of their diet.

Protein for Growth: For rabbits to grow strong and healthy, especially during the early growth stages, they need a protein source. Young rabbits benefit from a diet with a protein content of around 16–18%, while adult rabbits do well on about 12–14%.

Vitamins and Minerals: Fresh vegetables provide essential vitamins and minerals. Leafy greens like romaine lettuce, dandelion greens, and carrot tops are excellent choices, but avoid giving too many high-calcium greens, like spinach, as it can lead to kidney problems in rabbits.

Limited Carbohydrates: Rabbits are not built to process large amounts of sugars or carbohydrates. Treats like fruits should be given in moderation, as too much sugar can lead to obesity and other health issues.

2. Setting Up a Daily Feeding Schedule

Morning Feeding: Begin the day by providing fresh hay. This not only gives rabbits their needed fiber but also keeps them busy and engaged, which is helpful for their mental health. Give a measured amount of pellets according to the age and size of each rabbit.

Midday Fresh Veggies: Offer a small portion of fresh vegetables. Aim to give a variety of leafy greens to provide essential nutrients. Be mindful not to overfeed veggies to avoid digestive upset.

Evening Hay Replenishment and Water Check: Refill hay supplies if needed and check that water containers are clean and full. Clean, fresh water is vital as rabbits can become dehydrated easily, which impacts their overall health.

3. Adjusting the Schedule for Growth Stages

Kits (Baby Rabbits): Kits should stay with their mother until they are 6-8 weeks old, receiving nutrients from her milk. After weaning, gradually introduce hay and pellets, starting with higher protein content for growth.

Growing Rabbits (Up to 6 Months): At this stage, young rabbits require a protein-rich diet. Continue providing unlimited hay, along with measured portions of high-quality pellets and a small portion of fresh vegetables. Be consistent with feeding times to help them establish a routine.

Adult Rabbits: For rabbits over 6 months, switch to a lower-protein pellet and focus on providing ample fiber. Fresh vegetables should be given daily, with fruit only as an occasional treat. Maintaining a regular feeding schedule helps prevent obesity and digestive issues in adult rabbits.

Breeding Does and Bucks: Rabbits intended for breeding will have slightly different needs.

Breeding does, in particular, need more protein and energy during pregnancy and lactation. Providing extra pellets and leafy greens during these times supports both the mother and her kits.

4. Tips for Consistency and Health

Same Time Every Day: Rabbits are creatures of habit, and feeding at the same times each day helps them feel secure and keeps their digestive systems stable.

Clean, Fresh Food: Always check that food is fresh. Spoiled vegetables or damp hay can cause illness.

Monitor Intake and Health: Take note of any changes in appetite, weight, or droppings, as these can indicate health issues. If a rabbit suddenly stops eating, this can be an emergency in rabbits, as they are prone to digestive stasis.

5. Avoiding Common Feeding Mistakes

Avoid Overfeeding Pellets: Too many pellets can cause rabbits to gain weight and reduce their intake of hay, which is essential for digestion.

Limit Fruits and Sugary Foods: Even though rabbits enjoy fruits, these should only be given sparingly as treats. Examples include apple slices (without seeds) or small pieces of banana.

Introduce New Foods Gradually: When adding a new food item to their diet, introduce it slowly over several days to see how each rabbit reacts. Sudden changes in diet can lead to digestive problems.

By creating a structured feeding schedule, you're supporting the rabbits' natural growth, health, and productivity. Focus on high-fiber hay, balanced protein, and fresh vegetables, adjusting as needed for each growth stage. A consistent, well-planned feeding schedule not only helps each rabbit thrive but also improves the overall success of your backyard farming efforts.

Regularly monitoring and fine-tuning your approach will ensure your rabbits reach optimal health and growth, making your backyard rabbit farming both rewarding and sustainable.

Chapter 4

Breeding for Maximum Meat Production

4.1 Selecting Breeding Pairs

In backyard rabbit farming, selecting the right breeding pairs is essential for maximizing meat production. The choice of breeding pairs not only impacts the health and quality of the rabbits but also determines the overall efficiency of meat yield. To make breeding easier, it's important to focus on certain key traits in both does (females) and bucks (males) that align with the goal of a productive, sustainable meat rabbit operation.

1. Prioritize Size and Growth Rate

For meat production, size matters. Larger rabbits with strong growth rates typically yield more meat and mature faster, making them ideal for a meat-focused breeding program. When selecting breeding pairs, choose rabbits that consistently exhibit fast growth, reaching market weight (around 5 pounds) in 10 to 12 weeks. This growth rate not only shortens the time from birth to harvest but also reduces feeding costs, making your operation more efficient.

2. Select for Health and Hardiness

Healthy rabbits are the backbone of a successful breeding program. Look for breeding stock with a strong immune system, resilience to common diseases, and minimal veterinary needs. When selecting breeding pairs, observe for signs of robust health—clear eyes, a smooth, shiny coat, and strong energy levels. Hardy rabbits that can withstand varying weather conditions are especially valuable in backyard settings, where climate control may be limited.

3. Temperament Counts for Handling Ease

While temperament might not directly affect meat production, it plays a practical role in managing your rabbits. Calm, manageable rabbits are easier to handle, especially for routine care and breeding purposes. When selecting does and bucks, choose those with a docile, cooperative temperament. This trait can help minimize stress, making it easier to work with the rabbits and maintain a stable environment.

4. Consider Reproductive Performance and Litter Size

Does with a history of large, healthy litters and high survival rates are crucial in meat production, as they produce more offspring per breeding cycle. Ideally, choose does that consistently deliver 8-12 kits per litter and exhibit strong mothering instincts, ensuring that the young are well-cared for and have a higher survival rate. Bucks should also come from lines known for strong reproductive performance, as their genetics will influence the health and vitality of future litters.

5. Look for Good Meat-to-Bone Ratio

The meat-to-bone ratio is a key factor in maximizing meat yield. Some rabbit breeds and specific bloodlines are known for producing rabbits with more muscle and less bone. Select breeding pairs that carry genes for meatier builds—broad shoulders, a full loin, and rounded haunches indicate a higher yield. Such rabbits tend to have well-developed muscles, which contribute to a greater return on each animal raised.

6. Use Select Breeds Known for Meat Production

Certain rabbit breeds are better suited for meat production due to their growth rates and build. The most popular meat breeds include:

New Zealand: Known for rapid growth and a high meat-to-bone ratio, New Zealand rabbits are a staple for meat production.

Californian: Often crossed with New Zealand rabbits for hardiness and growth efficiency, Californians produce high-quality meat with excellent growth rates.

Flemish Giant: Though slower growing, they add size and body mass when crossbred, resulting in larger offspring.

When selecting breeding pairs, choose rabbits from proven meat breeds or hybrids that have been crossbred specifically for meat production.

7. Keep Detailed Breeding Records

Maintaining detailed records of each rabbit's growth, health, and reproductive performance is invaluable in making informed breeding decisions. Records allow you to track which pairs produce the healthiest, largest offspring and help identify any recurring issues. Over time, these records will guide you in refining your breeding program, ensuring each generation yields better meat production than the last.

Choosing the right breeding pairs is the foundation of efficient meat production in backyard rabbit farming. By prioritizing size, health, reproductive performance, and temperament, you create a sustainable breeding program that aligns with your meat production goals. With the right rabbits, a thoughtful approach, and consistent record-keeping, you can achieve a productive and profitable backyard rabbit farm.

4.2 Managing Breeding Cycles

Managing breeding cycles in backyard rabbit farming is essential for consistent meat production and the health of the herd. The process involves planning, timing, and care to ensure that rabbits breed at optimal intervals and produce healthy, fast-growing offspring.

1. Understanding Breeding Age and Selection

Rabbits are typically ready to breed by five to six months of age, though larger breeds may take a bit longer. Choosing strong, healthy rabbits as breeding stock is crucial, as the quality of the parents directly influences the quality of the offspring. Look for rabbits with a strong build, healthy coat, and a calm demeanor, as these traits can lead to faster growth rates and healthier kits (young rabbits).

2. Setting a Breeding Schedule

To maintain consistent meat production, establish a breeding schedule. Female rabbits (does) can be bred every 90 days, but this may vary depending on her health and recovery after each litter. Many farmers use a 42-day cycle, where does rest for two weeks after weaning their litter before breeding again. This approach balances frequent litters with necessary recovery time.

Sample 42-Day Cycle:

Day 1: Mate the doe.

Day 28-30: Prepare for birth; provide a nesting box.

Day 30: Doe gives birth.

Day 42: Kits begin weaning; doe rests for two weeks.

3. Caring for Pregnant and Nursing Does

Pregnant and nursing does require extra nutrition. Ensure they have ample food and water, focusing on high-quality hay, pellets, and fresh greens. Clean, dry nesting areas are critical to protect newborn kits from illness and cold. Providing extra bedding helps them feel secure and stay warm.

4. Managing Litters for Optimal Growth

Once kits are born, handle them gently to build trust and check for any health issues. Kits grow quickly, especially with a mother on a nutritious diet. At about 6-8 weeks, they can be weaned and transitioned to a diet that encourages steady growth.

5. Monitoring and Adjusting the Breeding Program

Keep records of each doe's breeding cycle, litter sizes, and kit survival rates. Noting any health issues or growth differences allows you to adjust the breeding program. By focusing on strong breeders and reducing stress on the rabbits, you can maximize meat production while maintaining a healthy, productive herd.

This system, when practiced with care, makes it easier to manage a sustainable backyard rabbit operation, ultimately leading to greater meat yield with efficient breeding practices.

4.3 Caring for Pregnant Does and Newborn Kits

Raising rabbits for meat is a sustainable, rewarding venture for those interested in self-sufficiency and ethical animal care. To achieve the goal of maximizing meat yield, it's essential to manage breeding cycles, care properly for pregnant does, and ensure newborn kits grow strong. This approach requires a balance of attention, basic skills, and understanding of the breeding process. **Here's how you can take your backyard rabbit farming to the next level by focusing on the essentials of caring for pregnant does and newborn kits.**

1. Recognizing and Supporting Pregnant Does

Once a doe is bred, it's crucial to monitor her for signs of pregnancy. Although some does show clear signs like a rounder belly, others may keep you guessing. Generally, it's safe to assume she is pregnant 12–14 days after breeding. Handle her gently and limit stress, as pregnant rabbits can be sensitive to changes.

Provide Proper Nutrition: Good nutrition is the foundation of successful breeding. During pregnancy, increase her daily food intake slightly to support her and the developing kits. Offer a balanced diet rich in high-quality hay (like alfalfa or timothy), fresh water, and a specially formulated pellet for pregnant and nursing does.

Safe, Comfortable Environment: A calm, quiet space is essential. Avoid loud noises or sudden movements around your pregnant doe. Set up her enclosure in a draft-free area with clean, dry bedding.

2. Preparing for Birth (Kindling)

Kindling, or giving birth, usually occurs about 28–32 days after breeding. In the days leading up to birth, provide the doe with a nesting box, as she'll begin "nesting" by gathering fur and other materials to make a warm, secure nest for her kits.

Setting Up the Nesting Box: Place the box in her enclosure about five days before her due date. Fill it with clean straw or hay, then let her pull fur from her body to create a soft lining. This natural instinct helps keep the newborns warm and safe.

Watch for Signs of Labor: A doe may act restless or spend extra time in the nesting box just before kindling. Keep an eye on her, but allow her to go through the process without interference.

3. Caring for Newborn Kits

Once the kits are born, the mother's natural instincts typically guide her care, but there are steps you can take to support their healthy development.

Monitor, But Do Not Disturb: Newborn kits are tiny, hairless, and rely entirely on the warmth of their mother and the nesting box. Avoid handling them in the first few days unless absolutely necessary, as disturbing them may cause the mother to feel stressed.

Ensure the Doe is Nursing: Most does nurse their kits once or twice daily, usually at night. Check the kits' bellies to ensure they appear rounded and well-fed. If they seem thin or weak, consult a veterinarian or experienced rabbit breeder, as hand-feeding may be needed in rare cases.

4. Weaning and Beyond

At around 4–6 weeks of age, the kits will start nibbling on solid food. Gradually, they'll transition to hay, pellets, and water alongside their mother's milk. By 8 weeks, they are usually ready to be weaned and can be moved to their own enclosure.

Separate by Gender: It's essential to separate male and female kits around 8–12 weeks to avoid early, accidental breeding.

Track Growth and Health: Weigh and assess each kit regularly to monitor growth. Strong, healthy kits are essential for achieving high meat yields, so be attentive to their nutrition and health.

5. Breeding Cycles for Maximum Meat Production

For consistent meat production, establish a planned breeding schedule that maintains the health of your breeding stock without overburdening them.

Allow Rest Periods: Over-breeding can exhaust does, which can lead to lower kit survival rates and poor overall health. Give each doe a rest period between litters to maintain her condition.

Rotate Breeding Stock: Keep a few breeding does to ensure a steady supply of kits while allowing individual does time to recover. This practice also prevents inbreeding and maintains genetic diversity in your herd.

Caring for pregnant does and newborn kits with intention and knowledge is key to successful backyard rabbit farming. By ensuring proper nutrition, a calm environment, attentive monitoring, and a well-thought-out breeding schedule, you can raise healthy rabbits that yield high-quality meat. This simple, attentive approach can make backyard rabbit farming a rewarding experience for you and ensure a sustainable, abundant meat supply for your family.

Chapter 5

Health and Wellness in Your Rabbitry

5.1 Common Diseases and Their Prevention

Raising rabbits in a backyard setting can be a rewarding experience, but it's essential to stay aware of common diseases and take preventative measures to keep your rabbits healthy. Early awareness and routine care can help prevent many health issues that might otherwise threaten your rabbitry's success. Here's a straightforward guide to common diseases in rabbits and practical steps to prevent them.

1. Pasteurellosis (Snuffles)

Cause: Bacterial infection (Pasteurella multocida).

Symptoms: Sneezing, nasal discharge, head shaking, swollen eyes, and breathing difficulties.

Prevention: Maintain clean housing, ensure good ventilation, and avoid overcrowding. Minimize stress by handling rabbits gently and keeping them in stable environments.

Treatment: Antibiotics are needed if infection occurs. Consult a veterinarian if symptoms appear.

2. Coccidiosis

Cause: Protozoan parasites affecting the liver or intestines.

Symptoms: Diarrhea, weight loss, lack of appetite, and bloated belly in severe cases.

Prevention: Keep hutches clean and dry. Sanitize food and water bowls regularly. Reduce wet or soiled bedding to limit parasite exposure.

Treatment: Immediate veterinary care with anti-parasitic medication is required. Good hydration and supportive care are essential.

3. Ear Mites

Cause: Parasitic mites (Psoroptes cuniculi) infecting the ear canal.

Symptoms: Shaking head, scratching ears, brown crusty discharge, and hair loss around the ears.

Prevention: Regularly inspect rabbits' ears for signs of mites. Maintain cleanliness in hutches and avoid contact with potentially infected animals.

Treatment: Topical anti-mite treatments are effective. Consult a vet for proper dosage and application.

4. Flystrike (Myiasis)

Cause: Flies laying eggs in soiled fur, with larvae feeding on the rabbit's flesh.

Symptoms: Restlessness, a strong odor, visible maggots in the fur, loss of appetite, and signs of distress.

Prevention: Keep rabbits and their bedding clean, especially in warmer months when flies are more active. Regularly inspect your rabbits for any sores or areas of matted fur where flies might lay eggs.

Treatment: Immediate veterinary intervention is crucial. Manually removing maggots and using prescribed medications can help, but this condition is an emergency.

5. GI Stasis (Gastrointestinal Stasis)

Cause: Slow or halted movement of food through the digestive tract, often due to diet changes, dehydration, or stress.

Symptoms: Lack of appetite, small or no droppings, hunched posture, and lethargy.

Prevention: Feed a high-fiber diet with plenty of hay to support gut health. Ensure rabbits have consistent access to clean water. Reduce stress by fostering a serene atmosphere.

Treatment: Seek veterinary care promptly, as GI stasis can be fatal if untreated. Rehydration, gentle massage, and medications may help stimulate digestion.

6. Overgrown Teeth (Malocclusion)

Cause: Teeth that grow improperly, often due to insufficient hay or genetic factors.

Symptoms: Drooling, difficulty eating, weight loss, and visibly misaligned teeth.

Prevention: Provide unlimited hay, which encourages natural tooth wear. Avoid selective breeding of rabbits with a history of malocclusion.

Treatment: A veterinarian can trim overgrown teeth as needed. Severe cases may require ongoing care or diet adjustments.

7. Heat Stress

Cause: Exposure to high temperatures without sufficient shade or ventilation.

Symptoms: Lethargy, panting, drooling, and lying stretched out.

Prevention: Provide shade and ensure proper ventilation in the rabbitry, especially in hot climates. Offer cool water, and use frozen water bottles for rabbits to lie against.

Treatment: Move the rabbit to a cool area, offer fresh water, and use a damp cloth on the ears. Contact a vet if symptoms persist.

Tips for Maintaining a Healthy Rabbitry

1. Regular Cleanliness: Clean hutches, feeders, and waterers frequently to reduce disease risks. Remove uneaten food promptly and replace soiled bedding.

2. Routine Health Checks: Look for any signs of illness, like changes in eating habits, droppings, or behavior. Early detection is key to successful treatment.

3. Balanced Diet: Feed high-quality hay, fresh water, and limited pellets, with occasional fresh greens. A healthy diet supports strong immunity and digestion.

4. Vaccinations and Vet Care: In some areas, vaccinations are available for diseases like rabbit hemorrhagic disease (RHD). Regular vet visits help address health issues early.

By understanding these common diseases and following preventive practices, you can help your rabbits thrive. Healthy rabbits grow faster, live longer, and ultimately provide greater returns, whether you're raising them for meat or as pets. Taking a proactive approach to rabbit wellness will make backyard rabbit farming more manageable and enjoyable.

5.2 Vaccinations and Veterinary Care

In backyard rabbit farming, maintaining health and wellness in your rabbitry is essential for a productive and successful operation. Rabbits are generally hardy animals, but proactive care, including vaccinations and veterinary support, can prevent common diseases and improve overall well-being.

Why Vaccinations Matter for Rabbits

Vaccinations can protect your rabbits from potentially deadly diseases, particularly if you live in an area where these diseases are common. **The two main illnesses that affect rabbits are Rabbit Hemorrhagic Disease (RHD) and Myxomatosis,** both of which can spread quickly and devastate a rabbitry.

Rabbit Hemorrhagic Disease (RHD): This viral disease affects the liver and other organs, often causing rapid death in affected rabbits. Vaccination is the best defense, especially if you live in a region where RHD is known to occur.

Myxomatosis: Spread by fleas, mosquitoes, and direct contact, this disease causes swelling, fever, and sometimes death. Vaccinating against Myxomatosis can be essential in certain areas.

Consulting with a veterinarian to determine the best vaccination schedule is crucial. Your vet will help you assess risk factors and suggest vaccinations based on your location, breed of rabbits, and specific conditions in your rabbitry.

Routine Health Checks

Regularly examining your rabbits is a simple yet effective way to catch health issues early. Look for signs of illness, such as:

Changes in eating habits

Weight loss or poor coat condition

Discharge from the eyes or nose

Lethargy or unusual behavior

Establishing a weekly routine to observe each rabbit can alert you to health concerns before they become serious.

Building a Relationship with a Veterinarian

Finding a veterinarian experienced in rabbit care is invaluable for guidance on disease prevention, treatment options, and general care tips. They can also assist with emergency situations, providing prompt care when needed.

Having a trusted vet who knows your rabbits' medical history can save time and increase the chances of successful treatments in cases of illness.

Tips for a Healthy Rabbitry

In addition to vaccinations and veterinary care, a few simple practices can help maintain a healthy environment:

Clean Housing: Regular cleaning of cages and living areas reduces the spread of disease.

Quarantine New Rabbits: When bringing new rabbits into your rabbitry, keep them isolated for a few weeks to ensure they're healthy and not carrying diseases.

Manage Stress Levels: Rabbits are sensitive animals, and minimizing stress (through proper handling and reducing overcrowding) can strengthen their immune systems.

Vaccinations, regular health checks, and a strong relationship with a veterinarian create a foundation of wellness in your rabbitry. By taking these steps, you help ensure your rabbits remain healthy, allowing you to focus on growing your rabbit farming venture with confidence and peace of mind.

5.3 Daily Care Practices to Ensure Health

Creating a healthy and thriving rabbitry starts with consistent daily care. Routine practices not only promote wellness but also prevent common health issues, making backyard rabbit farming a more manageable and rewarding experience.

1. Morning Check-In: Observing Your Rabbits

Every day, start by observing each rabbit for signs of good health or possible issues. Healthy rabbits are active, alert, and have clean, shiny fur. **Watch for:**

Clear, bright eyes without discharge

Clean noses, free of mucus

Smooth, firm bellies

Alert, calm behavior

Signs of illness can include lethargy, loss of appetite, labored breathing, or unusual behavior. Catching issues early can make a huge difference, so make this a daily habit.

2. Clean Water and Fresh Feed

Fresh water is essential and should be provided daily. Dirty water can lead to illnesses, so wash and refill water containers each morning. Check that the water supply is working properly if you use an automatic system, as clogged pipes or spouts can go unnoticed.

Alongside water, rabbits need a balanced diet for health. Hay is essential for digestion and should be available at all times. Daily feed should also include fresh greens (like leafy vegetables) and, if necessary, a small portion of high-quality pellets to ensure balanced nutrition. Avoid overfeeding pellets, as they can lead to obesity and digestive issues.

3. Litter Cleaning and Waste Management

Cleanliness is critical in a rabbitry. Each day, remove soiled litter from cages or hutches and replace it with fresh bedding. Clean litter areas prevent the spread of disease and reduce odor, making the environment more comfortable for both rabbits and handlers.

Collect rabbit droppings daily, as they make excellent compost for gardens. If using a tray system, empty and clean trays to minimize bacteria build-up and reduce health risks.

4. Exercise and Enrichment

Exercise is vital for both physical and mental health. Let rabbits out into an enclosed area where they can safely move around for a period each day. This relieves boredom and supports muscle and joint health. Provide chewing toys, tunnels, and simple obstacles to keep them stimulated and active.

5. Temperature and Environment Checks

Rabbits are sensitive to temperature extremes. Ensure they are sheltered from excessive heat and cold, especially if you live in a region with fluctuating temperatures. Daily checks on ventilation, shade, and the positioning of enclosures will help prevent heatstroke or hypothermia. Adding straw or blankets can help keep rabbits warm in colder weather.

6. Handling and Bonding

Gentle daily handling builds trust and makes it easier to inspect your rabbits for any health issues. Use these moments to check for lumps, injuries, or abnormalities. If rabbits are more comfortable with you, they'll be easier to handle in cases of emergency or when routine treatments are necessary.

7. Routine Grooming

Grooming is essential, especially for breeds with long hair, which can become matted if neglected. Daily brushing helps keep their coat clean and reduces the risk of hairballs, which can cause digestive blockages. For short-haired rabbits, grooming once a week may suffice, though daily observation will still be beneficial.

8. Monitoring Breeding Does and Growing Kits

If breeding, daily check on pregnant does and newly born kits. Make sure nesting areas are clean and kits are warm. Handling should be minimal with newborns, but visual checks are essential to confirm they are well-fed and thriving.

9. Documenting Health Observations

A daily log is a valuable tool for tracking each rabbit's health. Record observations, feeding amounts, and any notable behavior. This makes it easy to spot trends and anticipate potential issues before they escalate.

10. End-of-Day Wrap-Up

As evening approaches, do another brief inspection to ensure all rabbits are accounted for, fed, and comfortable. Check water levels, lock enclosures, and confirm they're safe from potential predators for the night.

By following these daily care practices, you set a strong foundation for healthy and happy rabbits. Regular routines not only prevent problems but also allow you to detect any early warning signs of illness. Healthy, well-cared-for rabbits grow better, live longer, and produce more consistently, making your rabbitry both productive and sustainable.

Chapter 6

Harvesting and Processing for Meat Yield

6.1 When and How to Harvest for Best Yield
Raising rabbits for meat in your backyard can be a rewarding way to provide fresh, high-quality protein. However, harvesting at the right time and processing correctly are key to maximizing yield and ensuring humane treatment. **Here's a comprehensive, straightforward guide on when and how to harvest for the best yield.**

1. When to Harvest

Timing Based on Age and Weight: The best time to harvest rabbits is typically between 8 to 12 weeks of age, depending on the breed. At this age, rabbits reach a mature weight, providing optimal meat yield while still being tender. Waiting longer can result in tougher meat, as the muscle fibers mature.

Breed-Specific Considerations: Different rabbit breeds grow at varying rates, so be sure to check the breed's growth timeline. Common meat breeds, like the New Zealand and Californian, are usually ready for harvest around 8 to 10 weeks. Slower-growing breeds may require a couple of extra weeks.

Health Status: Only healthy rabbits should be harvested. Check for any signs of illness before processing, as this affects both meat quality and safety. Any rabbits showing signs of disease should be examined by a veterinarian and either treated or removed from the meat cycle.

2. How to Harvest Humanely and Effectively

Preparation for Harvesting:

Calm Environment: Before harvesting, create a calm environment for the rabbit to reduce stress. Handling them gently in the days leading up to processing can help keep them relaxed.

Equipment: Ensure you have clean, sharp tools specifically designated for rabbit harvesting. Preparing in advance reduces the chance of complications and ensures a clean, quick process.

Humane Dispatching Methods:

Neck Dislocation (Cervical Dislocation): This is one of the most common methods used for humane dispatching. It's quick and, when done correctly, causes minimal distress to the rabbit.

Blunt Force Trauma: A quick blow to the back of the head can also be humane if done precisely, though it requires accuracy.

Other Methods: Some people use a "rabbit wringer" or a specialized tool that ensures humane dispatch. Always research and choose a method that aligns with both effectiveness and humane practices.

3. Processing for Maximum Meat Yield

Skinning and Dressing:

Start with Clean Equipment: Keep your knives and cutting surfaces sanitized. This reduces the risk of contamination, ensuring the meat stays fresh and safe.

Skinning Process: Make a small incision around the ankles, and peel back the skin with steady, gentle pressure. Using gravity by hanging the rabbit makes this easier.

Removing Organs: Carefully open the abdominal cavity to remove the organs. Many of these can be used or repurposed, adding to the overall yield.

Final Cleaning and Storage:

Rinse and Chill: Once the rabbit is skinned and gutted, rinse it in cold water to remove any remaining residue, then place it in an ice bath or refrigerator.

Packaging and Freezing: If not using the meat immediately, vacuum seal and freeze it to retain freshness. Proper packaging prevents freezer burn, keeping the meat in top condition.

4. Post-Harvest Processing Tips

Maximizing Use: Besides meat, rabbit by-products like the liver, kidneys, and even bones can be repurposed in soups, broths, or as pet food.

Record Keeping: Track harvest dates and weights to monitor yield over time. This information helps you improve practices for future harvests, refining your timing and techniques.

Harvesting rabbits for meat requires thoughtful planning and humane practices. By following these guidelines on when and how to harvest, you can achieve a sustainable yield that ensures both quality meat and ethical care for your rabbits.

6.2 Humane Slaughter and Processing

Raising backyard rabbits for meat can be rewarding and sustainable. However, humane slaughter and processing are crucial for ethical meat production, providing not only quality yield but also respecting the life of the animal. This guide walks you through each step, with clear instructions to keep the process manageable and respectful.

Preparing for Harvest

Before slaughter, ensure the rabbits are kept in a calm, clean, and quiet environment. Handle them gently in the days leading up to harvest, as stressed rabbits can have tougher meat and decreased quality. Withhold food for about 12 hours before processing, which helps ensure a cleaner system.

The Importance of a Quick, Painless Method

Choosing a humane method for slaughter is vital. The goal is to minimize the animal's stress and pain, preserving the integrity of the meat while respecting the rabbit's life. A quick, effective method commonly used by small-scale farmers is cervical dislocation, often referred to as the "broomstick" method. Properly done, this method is fast, minimizing suffering.

Processing the Rabbit

1. Bleeding the Animal: Once the rabbit is deceased, suspend it upside down by the hind legs and make a small incision in the neck to allow blood to drain. This step should be quick and clean to maintain meat quality.

2. Skinning: Start skinning by making incisions near the ankles, then work the hide downward toward the head. The hide should come off relatively smoothly; take your time to avoid puncturing the meat. Save the hide if you intend to use it for pelts.

3. Evisceration: This involves removing internal organs, which should be done carefully to prevent puncturing the intestines or stomach, as this can contaminate the meat. Use a sharp knife to open the body cavity along the belly, then gently pull out the organs. The liver, kidneys, and heart are edible and can be saved, while other parts can be composted or safely disposed of.

4. Rinsing and Chilling: Rinse the carcass thoroughly to remove any remaining blood and loose tissue, then place it in cold water to chill. This step helps firm up the meat and prevents spoilage. After chilling, rabbits can be processed further into cuts or left whole, depending on your preferences.

Storing and Using the Meat

For optimal quality, wrap and store rabbit meat in the freezer immediately after processing. Properly frozen, it can last several months.

Rabbit meat is lean, nutritious, and versatile, making it an excellent option for various recipes from stews to roasts.

Humane slaughter and careful processing not only enhance the quality of the meat but also maintain respect for the animal. Following these steps can make the process straightforward and rewarding, yielding healthy meat for you and your family. With thoughtful preparation, backyard rabbit raising can be a humane and sustainable way to add high-quality protein to your diet.

6.3 Meat Storage and Handling Tips

Proper storage and handling of rabbit meat after harvesting are essential for maintaining quality, safety, and flavor. **Here are some straightforward and effective tips to ensure that your hard-earned harvest lasts and provides nutritious, tender meat for your family.**

1. Cool the Meat Quickly

Once the rabbit is processed, it's important to bring the body temperature down as quickly as possible. Placing the meat in an ice-water bath immediately after processing helps slow bacterial growth. Ideally, let the meat stay in this ice bath for about 30 minutes to one hour, ensuring it is fully cooled.

2. Remove Excess Moisture

After cooling, remove the rabbit meat from the ice bath and pat it dry with clean paper towels or a cloth. Excess moisture can encourage bacterial growth, so it's essential to remove it. Dry meat also tends to freeze better, reducing the chance of freezer burn.

3. Portion the Meat for Convenient Use

Consider breaking down the meat into portions that suit your cooking needs before storing it. This makes meal prep easier and avoids repeatedly thawing and refreezing, which can degrade the meat's quality. For example, portion the meat into legs, loin sections, or stew-sized pieces, depending on how you plan to use it.

4. Vacuum Seal or Wrap Properly for Freezing

For longer storage, vacuum sealing is the best option, as it removes most air, slowing oxidation and preserving freshness. If you don't have a vacuum sealer, wrap each piece tightly in plastic wrap, followed by a layer of heavy-duty freezer paper or aluminum foil. Ensure the wrap is tight and that no air can seep in.

5. Label and Date Packages

Always label each package with the type of meat and the date it was processed. Rabbit meat can stay fresh in the freezer for up to a year, but it's best to use it within six to nine months for optimal taste and quality. Rotating your stock (using the oldest packages first) is a good practice to avoid spoilage.

6. Thaw Carefully to Preserve Texture

To thaw, place the meat in the refrigerator 24 hours before you plan to use it. This slow thawing process preserves texture and reduces the chance of bacterial growth. If you're in a hurry, you can thaw it in a bowl of cold water, but avoid thawing at room temperature, as this can lead to rapid bacterial growth on the surface.

7. Practice Good Hygiene Throughout

Handling rabbit meat requires attention to cleanliness. Always wash your hands, knives, and cutting surfaces before and after handling. Keeping your processing area clean and disinfected prevents contamination, ensuring your meat is safe to consume.

8. Use Fresh Meat Promptly or Store Safely

If you aren't planning to freeze the meat, keep it in the refrigerator and use it within 48 hours.

Rabbit meat is lean, which means it can dry out and lose quality quickly when not stored properly. By following these steps, you ensure it stays fresh and safe to eat.

By carefully storing and handling rabbit meat, you retain its nutritional value, flavor, and tenderness. A little extra care in storage can make a significant difference in the quality of the meat when it reaches your plate, ensuring that you get the most from your backyard harvest.

Chapter 7

Maximizing Profit in Rabbit Farming

7.1 Selling Rabbit Meat: Markets and Pricing

Selling rabbit meat offers a unique opportunity for small-scale farmers to tap into an expanding market that values locally sourced, sustainable protein options. To make rabbit farming profitable, it's essential to understand the best markets and determine fair, competitive pricing. Here's a breakdown of how to approach each area effectively.

1. Identifying Target Markets

Rabbit meat is versatile and appeals to niche markets. Start by identifying which segments to target. Common market types include:

Farmers' Markets: Many consumers seek healthier, organic meat at local farmers' markets. Setting up a stand allows you to sell directly, creating a relationship with customers who value local, fresh meat.

Restaurants and Chefs: Upscale or specialty restaurants often look for unique ingredients. Rabbit is seen as a delicacy, and chefs can be interested in buying directly from farmers for its quality.

Ethnic Communities: Some cultural groups have a tradition of eating rabbit and are familiar with cooking it. Research local demographics to locate communities that may already have a demand.

Health-Conscious Consumers: Rabbit meat is low in fat and high in protein, attracting health-focused consumers. You might reach these buyers directly through online sales, home delivery, or specialty food markets.

2. Setting a Competitive Price

Pricing can make or break your profitability, so setting the right price is crucial. **Here's how to determine it:**

Production Costs: Calculate the cost of raising each rabbit, including feed, housing, healthcare, and processing. These costs should be covered in your base price to ensure you don't operate at a loss.

Market Rates: Research what other local producers are charging. Farmers' market prices may be higher than wholesale prices to restaurants or retail stores.

Value-Added Products: In some cases, you may want to sell processed or pre-seasoned rabbit cuts. These products often fetch higher prices but require additional effort in packaging and possibly complying with food regulations.

Pricing Strategy: Consider different pricing for whole rabbits, half portions, and cuts like legs or loins. Each option can meet different customer needs and allow for flexibility in pricing.

3. Marketing Your Product

In addition to knowing your market and setting prices, effective marketing helps increase sales and customer loyalty. Highlight benefits like the sustainability of rabbit meat and its health advantages compared to other meats. Create simple, attractive labels, and consider offering recipes or cooking tips to encourage sales. A strong online presence, even with a simple website or social media page, can increase visibility and attract customers.

4. Building Customer Relationships

To retain customers, focus on building relationships. Consistency in quality, fair pricing, and personal engagement make a significant impact. Loyalty programs or discounts for repeat customers, and delivering orders punctually, can enhance customer trust and increase repeat purchases.

Selling rabbit meat for profit involves understanding market demands, accurately pricing based on costs and competition, and maintaining a marketing strategy that emphasizes quality and sustainability. By focusing on these elements, you can effectively maximize profit and sustain your rabbit farming business.

7.2 Additional Revenue Streams (Pelts, Manure, etc.)

When raising rabbits for meat production, maximizing profit means exploring every possible source of revenue. In addition to selling meat, there are several valuable by-products that can open up additional income streams, each adding to the farm's profitability. These include pelts, manure, and even creative uses for other rabbit products. **Here's how these revenue streams can support a more sustainable and profitable rabbit farming venture.**

1. Pelts: A Market for Rabbit Fur

Rabbit pelts, or skins, are an excellent source of additional income for farmers who want to expand their product offerings. With their soft, warm fur, rabbit pelts have a high demand in markets for clothing, accessories, and home goods.

How to Start with Pelts:

Breeding for Quality Fur: Certain rabbit breeds, such as Rex and Angora, are especially valued for their high-quality pelts. Choose breeds carefully if selling pelts is a significant revenue goal.

Processing and Preservation: Properly processing pelts after harvesting is essential. This includes careful skinning, cleaning, and curing to maintain fur quality. Some farmers choose to work with tanneries for professional processing.

Targeting Markets: Rabbit pelts can be sold directly to artisans, craft makers, or clothing companies. Farmers may also find local markets, online marketplaces, or niche communities interested in these natural materials.

2. Manure: An Organic Fertilizer

Rabbit manure is considered one of the best natural fertilizers. It's nutrient-rich and does not need composting before use, unlike other livestock manure. This makes it an ideal product for gardeners and farmers looking for a high-quality organic fertilizer.

Making Money with Rabbit Manure:

Packaging and Selling: Rabbit manure can be sold fresh or in dried pellet form. Many small farms package manure in bags for sale at farmers' markets, gardening stores, or through online platforms.

Bulk Sales to Gardeners and Farmers: Local gardeners, landscapers, and organic farms may be interested in buying rabbit manure in bulk. It's particularly valued for growing vegetables and flowers because it enriches the soil naturally.

Composting Services: Offering pre-composted rabbit manure can add further value for customers. Composting manure before sale can enhance its nutrient availability, creating a premium product that's easy for customers to use.

3. Other By-products: Pet Food and Animal Treats

Beyond pelts and manure, rabbit farmers can explore other profitable uses for by-products, such as organs, bones, and trimmings. These can be processed and sold as natural pet food, treats, or supplements for other animals.

Ways to Utilize By-products:

Pet Food and Treats: Rabbit meat, including organs, is highly nutritious and often used in premium pet foods. By turning excess or unused meat into raw pet food or treats, farmers can access the booming pet industry.

Animal Supplements: Rabbit parts like ears, feet, or bones can be sold as natural chew toys for dogs or enrichment treats for other animals. These products are especially appealing to pet owners looking for all-natural options.

Custom Orders: Some pet owners or animal shelters seek specific rabbit parts for dietary needs. Custom orders can add another layer of income, allowing farmers to provide specialized products to niche markets.

4. Rabbit Fiber: Wool for Knitting and Crafting

If the farm raises Angora rabbits, their wool offers another profitable by-product. Angora wool is incredibly soft, warm, and highly sought after by knitters and crafters.

Selling Rabbit Wool:

Harvesting and Care: Angora rabbits require regular grooming, and wool can be harvested through shearing or combing. Farmers should ensure gentle, humane handling to maintain the wool's quality.

Marketing to Crafters and Artisans: Angora wool can be sold raw, spun into yarn, or used in handmade products like scarves or hats. Many artisans appreciate the unique qualities of Angora wool and may be willing to pay a premium for quality fiber.

Joining Craft Markets: Farmers can tap into craft fairs, fiber festivals, and online platforms for wool and fiber enthusiasts to sell Angora wool and products directly.

5. Educational Workshops and Farm Tours

Lastly, rabbit farming knowledge can also become an income source. Educational workshops, farm tours, or online classes can attract people interested in learning more about sustainable agriculture and homesteading.

How to Create Learning Experiences:

Hosting On-site Farm Tours: Offering guided tours that explain rabbit care, breeding, and sustainable practices can be an engaging experience for visitors.

Educational Workshops: Teaching skills such as pelt processing, composting manure, or Angora wool spinning can be a profitable way to share expertise.

Virtual Learning Options: Virtual workshops or video content allow rabbit farmers to reach audiences beyond their local area, adding a flexible revenue stream to the business.

Making the Most of Every Resource

By diversifying income with these additional revenue streams, rabbit farmers can make full use of their resources and increase profitability. Each of these revenue streams—pelts, manure, pet products, wool, and educational experiences—requires time, effort, and a market-savvy approach. However, they offer excellent opportunities for farmers to create a sustainable, profitable business by maximizing the value of every part of their rabbit operation.

7.3 Building a Customer Base and Marketing Your Rabbits

Building a customer base and effectively marketing your rabbits are essential to running a profitable rabbit farming business. With the right strategies, you can establish loyal customers and reach new markets, ensuring your farm thrives. **Here's a clear, straightforward guide to building and growing a customer base for your rabbit products.**

1. Understanding Your Market

Know Your Customers: Identify who would be interested in your rabbits. Are they chefs, health-conscious consumers, local grocery stores, pet owners, or other farmers? Each group has different needs, and understanding them helps you tailor your marketing.

Research Demand and Trends: Look at trends in your area and beyond. Rabbit meat, for instance, is lean and high in protein, appealing to those seeking healthy alternatives to traditional meats. If you're selling rabbits as pets, focus on local pet stores, individual buyers, or online platforms.

2. Developing a Brand

Create a Unique Selling Proposition (USP): This is what makes your rabbits and your farm different. Your USP could highlight humane treatment, organic feeding practices, or family-farmed values. For example, you might market your rabbits as "naturally raised for a leaner, tastier product."

Establish Your Reputation: Ensure high standards in quality, care, and customer service. Satisfied customers often become repeat buyers and refer others, so prioritize their experience with your product and service.

3. Marketing Your Rabbits

Online Marketing: Use a website or social media platforms like Instagram, Facebook, or YouTube to showcase your rabbits and the story behind your farm. Share photos, videos, and updates about your breeding practices, health protocols, and the benefits of rabbit meat or pets. Highlighting your personal touch and ethical practices builds trust and customer interest.

Local Marketing: Attend farmers' markets, agricultural fairs, or local events. Personal connections made at these venues can often lead to loyal customers. Set up a booth with clear, attractive signage and samples if possible, allowing customers to experience your product firsthand.

Collaborate with Local Businesses: Partner with restaurants or health food stores to feature your rabbit products on their menus or shelves. If customers can try your rabbit meat in local dishes, they may be more inclined to buy directly from you.

4. Building Customer Loyalty

Consistent Communication: Use newsletters or social media to keep customers informed of new products, seasonal availability, or special offers. For instance, a monthly newsletter could share recipes, cooking tips, or news from the farm.

Rewards for Repeat Customers: Offer discounts, loyalty programs, or special deals for frequent buyers. A "buy three, get one free" offer for rabbit meat can encourage more purchases and build loyalty.

Listen to Feedback: Keep communication open and be responsive to customer feedback. Improving your service or addressing issues quickly can turn a one-time buyer into a long-term customer.

5. Expanding Your Reach

Use Online Marketplaces: Consider listing your rabbits or products on online marketplaces if local demand is limited. Sites like Craigslist, Facebook Marketplace, or specialized agricultural platforms can help you reach a broader audience.

Approach Niche Markets: Targeting specific markets, such as high-end restaurants or organic grocery stores, can help you command a higher price for your rabbits. Chefs looking for unique and sustainable meat options may be particularly interested in what you offer.

Invest in High-Quality Packaging: If you're shipping rabbit meat, quality packaging that preserves freshness and meets health regulations is essential. Clear labeling and professional presentation can make a lasting impression on customers and add value to your product.

6. Setting Fair Pricing

Calculate Your Costs Carefully: Understand all expenses involved in raising, processing, and marketing your rabbits, from feed and housing to transportation. Price your product to cover costs and leave room for a fair profit margin.

Research Local and Online Prices: Get an idea of what similar products are priced at in your area and online. Competing in price can be effective, but if your product is unique, don't be afraid to charge more for higher quality.

Offer Value-Based Pricing: If your rabbits are raised with special care, marketed as hormone-free or organic, or come with high-quality packaging, emphasize these qualities in your marketing and adjust your pricing accordingly.

Building a customer base and marketing your rabbits are critical steps in maximizing profit in rabbit farming. By understanding your market, developing a strong brand, and maintaining high-quality standards, you'll create value that customers appreciate. Effective marketing helps attract new buyers, and offering exceptional service keeps them coming back. With dedication and a strategic approach, your rabbit farm can grow into a profitable and respected business.

Chapter 8

Scaling Up Your Rabbitry for Higher Yield

8.1 Expanding Housing and Herd Size

Raising rabbits in your backyard can be a rewarding experience, both as a hobby and a source of additional income. However, once you've gained experience and confidence in managing a small rabbitry, you might find yourself thinking about scaling up. Expanding your rabbit farm can significantly increase your yield, whether you're raising rabbits for meat, fur, or as breeding stock. But before you dive into expansion, it's important to plan carefully. This ensures you avoid common pitfalls and grow your rabbitry in a sustainable way.

Why Expand Your Rabbitry?

Expanding your operation can provide several benefits:

1. Increased Meat or Fur Production: With more rabbits, you can produce larger quantities of meat or fur, allowing you to sell to more customers or meet higher demands in your community.

2. Improved Breeding Programs: A larger herd size gives you more genetic diversity, which can improve the health and productivity of your herd over time.

3. Greater Income Potential: More rabbits mean more products to sell, whether it's meat, fur, or live rabbits for breeding, which can boost your income.

Key Considerations Before Expanding

Before increasing the number of rabbits you raise, there are several key factors to consider. Expanding too quickly or without proper planning could lead to problems, such as overcrowding, increased disease, and higher costs.

1. Space and Housing

The first thing to consider is whether you have enough space. Rabbits require adequate room to thrive, and overcrowding can lead to stress, disease, and lower productivity. Each rabbit needs a clean, well-ventilated, and secure living space. When expanding, you will need to build or buy more hutches or cages.

Here are some guidelines for housing:

Size: Each adult rabbit should have at least 4-6 square feet of space. For breeding does (female rabbits), larger cages are preferable, especially when they have litters.

Ventilation: Good airflow is essential to prevent respiratory issues. Ensure that cages are well-ventilated but still protect rabbits from drafts.

Security: Properly secure housing will protect your rabbits from predators such as dogs, raccoons, or hawks.

Cleanliness: Make sure you have enough time and resources to clean the expanded housing regularly to prevent the buildup of waste and minimize disease risks.

2. Feeding and Watering

As you expand your rabbitry, your feed and water needs will also increase. Rabbits need a balanced diet of hay, pellets, and fresh greens. Expanding your herd could drive up feed costs, so it's important to plan for this.

Storage: You will need a place to store the increased amount of feed, ensuring it stays dry and free from pests.

Watering System: Consider upgrading to an automatic watering system if you haven't already. This will save time and ensure that all your rabbits have constant access to fresh, clean water.

3. Breeding and Herd Management

When you expand your rabbitry, you'll likely increase the number of breeding pairs. Managing a larger herd requires careful planning to avoid inbreeding and to maintain healthy genetic diversity.

Breeding Records: Keep detailed records of each rabbit's lineage, breeding history, and health. This will help you make informed decisions about which rabbits to breed and when.

Culling: As your herd grows, you will need to be selective about which rabbits you keep for breeding and which ones you cull (remove from the breeding program). Only breed rabbits with strong genetics, good temperaments, and high productivity.

4. Health and Disease Management

With more rabbits comes a higher risk of disease outbreaks. It's crucial to have a plan in place to manage the health of your herd.

Quarantine: When introducing new rabbits to your herd, quarantine them for at least 30 days to ensure they don't introduce diseases.

Regular Health Checks: Expand your routine health checks to catch any signs of illness early. Watch for symptoms such as lethargy, weight loss, or respiratory issues.

Veterinary Support: As your rabbitry grows, it's a good idea to establish a relationship with a vet who has experience with rabbits. They can help with routine health care and emergencies.

5. Time and Labor

Managing a larger rabbitry requires more time and effort. Feeding, cleaning, and health checks will take longer as your herd grows. Before expanding, assess whether you have enough time to properly care for the extra rabbits or if you need to hire additional help.

Steps to Expand Your Rabbitry

Once you've considered the key factors, you can begin expanding your rabbitry in a structured way. **Here's a general outline of how to scale up:**

1. Assess Your Current Setup: Evaluate your current housing, feeding, and management systems. Identify what needs to be upgraded or expanded.

2. Plan Your Expansion: Decide how many rabbits you want to add and how quickly you want to scale up. Make sure you have the resources to support the growth.

3. Build or Purchase Additional Housing: Start by expanding your housing and making sure you have enough space for the new rabbits.

4. Introduce New Rabbits Gradually: Don't add too many rabbits at once. Start with a few new breeding pairs and gradually increase your herd size.

5. Improve Your Systems: As you expand, streamline your feeding, watering, and cleaning systems to save time and reduce labor.

Expanding your rabbitry can be a great way to increase your yield and profits, but it requires careful planning and management. By ensuring you have enough space, maintaining proper feeding and health systems, and managing your breeding program carefully, you can successfully scale up your operation. Keep in mind that the health and well-being of your rabbits should always come first. A healthy herd will lead to a more productive and profitable rabbitry in the long term.

By thinking through these factors and expanding methodically, you'll be well on your way to running a successful, larger-scale backyard rabbit farm.

8.2 Cost Analysis for Scaling Profitably

Backyard rabbit farming can be a highly rewarding venture, both as a hobby and as a profitable business. However, like any business, success hinges on careful planning and understanding the financial implications of scaling your operation. If you want to expand your rabbit farming for profit, performing a detailed cost analysis is crucial. This will help you avoid unnecessary expenses and ensure that your growth is sustainable. In this guide, we'll break down the costs involved and how to manage them as you scale up.

Key Costs to Consider in Rabbit Farming

When analyzing the costs of scaling your backyard rabbit farming business, you need to consider several different areas. These can be grouped into start-up costs, operational costs, and scaling costs.

1. Start-up Costs

These are the initial costs you'll need to cover as you begin your rabbit farming operation. If you're already farming on a small scale, these expenses might be familiar, but they will increase as you scale.

Housing (hutches or cages): Rabbits need secure, comfortable housing that protects them from the elements and predators. For a small operation, you may only need a few cages, but as you scale, you'll need to build or buy more. Each hutch or cage could range from $25 to $150 depending on the material and size.

Breeding Stock: The cost of purchasing your initial breeding stock can vary depending on the breed and location. Each rabbit can cost between $20 and $50. As you scale, you'll need to increase the number of breeding pairs to maintain your production rate.

Feeders and Waterers: These are essential for supplying food and water to your rabbits efficiently. High-quality feeders and waterers can cost $10 to $30 each. As your operation grows, you'll need to buy more of these supplies.

Permits and Licensing (if applicable): Depending on your location, you may need to acquire permits or licenses to operate a farm, especially as you expand. The cost of these permits varies, so it's important to research local regulations.

2. Operational Costs

These are ongoing costs that you'll incur regularly, and they tend to increase with the number of rabbits you raise. In a scaled-up operation, managing these costs efficiently is key to maintaining profitability.

Feed: Rabbits require a balanced diet, and feed is one of the largest recurring expenses in rabbit farming. On average, a rabbit consumes about ¼ to ½ pound of feed per day, which will cost about $20 to $40 per month per rabbit. As you expand, bulk buying could reduce costs per unit, but the total feed cost will still rise with the number of rabbits.

Bedding and Cleaning Supplies: Keeping your rabbit hutches clean is essential for their health. Bedding materials like straw or wood shavings are another ongoing expense. Depending on the size of your operation, this could cost $10 to $50 per month.

Veterinary Care: Regular health checks and vaccinations are important to reduce the risk of disease outbreaks, especially as you increase the number of rabbits. Budgeting for periodic vet visits and medications is crucial. These costs can range from $50 to $200 annually, depending on the size of your herd and local veterinary rates.

Electricity and Water: If you're using electric heaters, fans, or automatic watering systems, your utility bills will increase as you scale. The cost will vary depending on your region, but it's important to account for higher water and electricity usage.

3. Scaling Costs

Once your operation moves beyond a small backyard setup, you'll need to invest in additional infrastructure and tools to manage the increased workload efficiently.

Expansion of Housing: As your rabbit population grows, you'll need to expand housing. This could mean building more hutches, or even constructing a larger barn or shelter. Costs for expanding housing can range from $500 to $5,000, depending on the scale and materials.

Breeding Management: As you scale, you'll need a more organized system for managing your breeding cycles. This could involve purchasing additional breeding stock to ensure you maintain consistent production. You might also need to invest in record-keeping tools or software to track breeding schedules, health records, and inventory.

Labor Costs: At some point, managing a larger number of rabbits may require additional labor. You might need to hire part-time help or family members to assist with daily tasks. Labor costs can vary significantly, but even part-time help could add several hundred dollars per month to your expenses.

Marketing and Sales: Expanding your farm will likely require you to invest in marketing if you want to sell your rabbits or rabbit products (like meat, fur, or manure) at scale. You might need to create a website, advertise on social media, or attend local farmers' markets. These marketing activities could cost anywhere from

$100 to $500 per month, depending on your strategy.

Strategies for Scaling Profitably

Scaling your backyard rabbit farm can be profitable, but only if you manage your costs effectively and find ways to increase your revenue. Here are some strategies to ensure profitability:

1. Economies of Scale
As you scale, take advantage of bulk purchasing. Buying feed, bedding, and other supplies in larger quantities can reduce your costs per unit. Work with local suppliers or co-ops to negotiate better prices for large orders.

2. Diversify Revenue Streams
Look for ways to diversify your income beyond just selling rabbits. For example, you could sell rabbit manure as fertilizer, rabbit pelts for crafts, or even offer workshops on rabbit farming. This

will help you maximize the profitability of each rabbit you raise.

3. Optimize Breeding Cycles

Effective management of your breeding cycles is critical to scaling profitably. Ensure that your does (female rabbits) are breeding consistently but not overbred, which can lead to health problems. A healthy doe can produce up to five litters a year, depending on the breed, but it's important to monitor their health and adjust accordingly.

4. Reduce Waste

Minimizing waste is one of the easiest ways to increase profitability. Ensure that feed is stored properly to prevent spoilage, and closely monitor your rabbits' health to avoid costly vet bills. Efficient use of bedding and water can also help you cut costs.

5. Focus on Quality

Whether you're selling rabbits for meat, breeding stock, or pets, focusing on quality will help you command higher prices. Healthy, well-bred rabbits will attract more buyers and allow you to scale without cutting corners on care.

Scaling a backyard rabbit farm for profit requires careful planning and cost management. By understanding the different costs involved and implementing strategies to manage them, you can grow your operation sustainably. Keep in mind that every dollar saved or earned through efficiency and smart decisions will contribute to your long-term profitability. Focus on quality, minimize waste, and take advantage of economies of scale to ensure your rabbit farming business thrives as it grows.

Chapter 9

Troubleshooting Common Challenges

9.1 Addressing Poor Growth and Low Yield

Backyard rabbit farming can be rewarding, both for personal use and small-scale profit. But when growth or yield falls short, it's essential to understand and address the root causes. This guide simplifies common challenges and offers practical solutions to improve your rabbits' health, growth, and overall meat yield.

1. Nutritional Deficiencies

Problem: Rabbits need a balanced diet to thrive. Poor nutrition can slow growth, reduce weight gain, and affect overall health.

Solution: Ensure a diet rich in high-quality hay, clean water, and pellet feed designed for rabbits. Adding fresh greens (such as leafy vegetables) and a source of protein can also boost growth.

Always avoid overfeeding sugary treats, as this can lead to digestive issues.

2. Poor Housing and Sanitation

Problem: Dirty or overcrowded cages cause stress and disease, both of which harm growth and productivity.

Solution: Keep cages clean, well-ventilated, and spacious enough for each rabbit to move comfortably. Regularly clean bedding and remove waste, which prevents infections. Ensure cages are dry and free from drafts while maintaining good airflow.

3. Genetic Issues

Problem: Some rabbits may have genetic traits that naturally limit growth or productivity.

Solution: Choose breeding pairs with proven growth records. Select rabbits from strong, healthy lines known for their robust growth and good yield. By improving your breeding program, you can gradually improve the quality and productivity of your stock.

4. Health and Disease

Problem: Illnesses and parasites, such as coccidiosis or mites, can stunt growth and reduce yield.

Solution: Monitor your rabbits for any signs of disease—like lethargy, loss of appetite, or unusual droppings—and address issues immediately. Consult a vet when needed. Regularly deworm your rabbits and provide vaccinations as necessary. Routine checks can help prevent health issues from spreading throughout the rabbitry.

5. Stress and Environmental Factors

Problem: Rabbits are sensitive animals, and high-stress environments slow growth and reduce reproduction rates.

Solution: Maintain a calm environment, away from loud noises or frequent disruptions. If temperatures are extreme, provide shade and cooling in summer and warmth in winter. Avoid sudden changes in diet or habitat, as these stress rabbits and affect growth.

6. Breeding and Reproduction Management

Problem: Poor breeding practices, such as breeding rabbits too young or too frequently, reduce the health and productivity of does (female rabbits).

Solution: Allow rabbits to reach maturity before breeding and space breeding cycles to give does recovery time. Careful management of breeding schedules ensures both higher yield and healthier offspring, which will be more likely to grow quickly and reach optimal weight.

7. Water and Hydration Issues

Problem: Rabbits need constant access to clean water for proper digestion, metabolism, and growth. Dehydration stunts growth and affects overall health.

Solution: Check water supplies daily to ensure fresh, clean water is available. Use drip bottles or non-tip bowls that are easy to clean. Hydration is especially crucial during warmer months, so monitor intake and adjust if rabbits appear to be drinking less.

Addressing these common issues can make a significant difference in the growth rate and yield of backyard rabbits. By understanding your rabbits' needs and maintaining a high standard of care, you're setting up a healthier, more productive rabbitry. Thoughtful and consistent management will not only improve growth rates but also contribute to a more enjoyable and rewarding rabbit-farming experience.

9.2 Managing Stress and Behavioral Issues

Managing stress and behavioral issues in backyard rabbit farming can be a crucial part of creating a successful, humane, and profitable operation. Rabbits are generally gentle animals, but like all creatures, they can be sensitive to changes in their environment and may develop stress-related behaviors that could affect their health, growth, and productivity. **Here's a clear, effective approach to troubleshooting common challenges in managing rabbit stress and behavioral issues.**

1. Understanding Rabbit Stress Triggers

Rabbits, being prey animals, are naturally alert and can be easily startled. **Common stress triggers in rabbits include:**

Environmental changes: Sudden shifts in temperature, light, or cage location can make rabbits anxious.

Noise: Loud sounds, such as nearby machinery or barking dogs, can induce stress.

Handling: Frequent or rough handling, especially if done incorrectly, can frighten rabbits and make them defensive.

Social dynamics: Rabbits are social but territorial. Housing them too close without adequate space or placing unfamiliar rabbits together can lead to fights.

Reducing these stressors is key to maintaining calm and content rabbits. Maintaining consistent environmental conditions, controlling noise levels, handling rabbits gently, and giving each rabbit adequate space can go a long way in preventing stress-related behaviors.

2. Common Stress-Related Behaviors and Solutions

When stressed, rabbits might display certain behaviors, including:

Thumping: Rabbits stomp their hind legs when they feel threatened. If a rabbit thumps frequently, identify any nearby noise or potential predator that might be causing alarm.

Aggression: Rabbits may bite, scratch, or lunge when they feel cornered or afraid. To reduce this, make sure the rabbits have personal space, handle them calmly, and avoid sudden movements.

Bar Chewing: This can be a sign of boredom, stress, or inadequate diet. Providing enrichment toys, like untreated wood blocks, and ensuring a well-rounded diet can alleviate this behavior.

Regular observation helps identify these behaviors early so that you can act quickly to remove stressors or provide solutions.

3. Providing a Calm, Enriching Environment

A calm environment is essential in managing stress and promoting good behavior in rabbits.

Here are practical ways to ensure their space promotes well-being:

Temperature and Ventilation Control: Keep the area ventilated and maintain a steady temperature, especially during extreme weather. Shade or insulation during hot summers and proper bedding during winters are beneficial.

Space and Shelter: Ensure each rabbit has adequate space to move and hide. Adding a small, covered area in each cage can offer a sense of security, giving them a place to retreat if they feel uneasy.

Mental and Physical Stimulation: Rabbits thrive with mental engagement. Place toys, tubes, and hay inside their cages to provide enrichment and prevent boredom, which can reduce stress-induced behaviors.

4. Addressing Behavioral Problems

Addressing behavioral problems involves understanding their root causes and using patient, humane methods to resolve them. Some common behavioral issues and approaches to address them are:

Fighting: If rabbits fight, particularly if they're housed close together, it may mean they're uncomfortable with each other. Ideally, introduce rabbits slowly and only if they are compatible. If aggression persists, house them separately.

Spraying or Marking: Unneutered rabbits often spray to mark their territory. Neutering can help reduce marking behaviors, making it easier to keep their environment clean and reduce territorial aggression.

Digging and Destruction: Rabbits naturally dig and chew. Giving them an outlet, like a dedicated area to dig or chew-safe toys, can channel this behavior positively.

5. Regular Check-ups and Health Monitoring

Often, stress behaviors in rabbits stem from underlying health issues. A rabbit in pain or discomfort may show aggression, isolation, or restlessness. Regularly examine your rabbits for signs of illness, injury, or discomfort. Having a veterinarian assess your rabbits periodically can catch health issues early before they worsen or lead to stress behaviors.

Managing stress and behavioral issues in backyard rabbit farming is not just about controlling the animals but creating an environment that meets their needs. By understanding rabbit behavior, providing a secure and stimulating habitat, and recognizing early signs of stress, you can maintain a harmonious rabbitry where rabbits are productive and healthy. Happy, well-cared-for rabbits are less likely to experience stress and are more likely to thrive, leading to better growth rates, healthier litters, and a more profitable operation overall.

9.3 Preventing Losses and Maximizing Efficiency

Backyard rabbit farming, when well-managed, can be a rewarding and efficient venture. But even with careful planning, challenges may arise. This section aims to equip you with straightforward troubleshooting strategies to handle common issues that can affect rabbit health, productivity, and your overall operation.

1. Understanding Health-Related Losses

Illness and Disease Prevention: Health issues are a major cause of loss. Simple biosecurity practices like regular cage cleaning, quarantining new or sick animals, and maintaining vaccination schedules can significantly reduce disease risks.

Recognizing Early Signs of Illness: Rabbits often hide their symptoms until the illness is advanced. Learn to observe changes in eating, drinking, grooming, and overall activity. Quick intervention with a vet can save lives and prevent the spread of disease.

Managing Heat Stress: Rabbits are sensitive to heat. Shade, good ventilation, and cool water bottles can prevent heatstroke in warmer months, especially if you live in a hot climate.

2. Optimizing Feed and Water Management

Providing Balanced Nutrition: Poor diet affects growth, reproduction, and meat quality. Ensure your rabbits receive the right balance of hay, pellets, fresh greens, and clean water daily.

Avoiding Feed Wastage: Wasting feed increases costs. Use feeders designed to minimize spillage and monitor how much food rabbits consume to adjust portions as needed.

3. Improving Breeding and Litter Management

Breeding Consistency: Efficient breeding schedules prevent gaps in production. Use breeding charts and keep accurate records to stay on track. Pairing rabbits with compatible temperaments also leads to better outcomes.

Litter Care: Proper litter management improves survival rates. Make sure nest boxes are warm, clean, and safe from overcrowding. Check kits regularly, as young rabbits can sometimes fall out of the nest or get injured by larger kits.

4. Handling Infrastructure Challenges

Proper Cage Design: Efficient cages minimize the risk of escape, injury, and disease. Ensure cages are the right size, sturdy, and have good ventilation. Use materials that are easy to clean and resistant to rust and wear.

Waste Management: Good waste management reduces odors and minimizes fly infestations. Frequent cleaning, along with a setup that keeps urine and droppings away from food, water, and nesting areas, keeps rabbits healthy and reduces maintenance time.

5. Avoiding Common Operational Pitfalls

Record-Keeping: Poor records lead to inefficiencies. Tracking breeding, health, and feed data helps you spot trends and make informed decisions that optimize costs and output.

Scaling Responsibly: Growing too quickly can lead to overcrowding, shortages of food, and labor challenges. Scale gradually so that you can maintain high standards of care and control costs.

By focusing on these core areas, you'll be well-prepared to handle common challenges in backyard rabbit farming, reducing losses and increasing both your efficiency and profitability.

Chapter 10

Building a Sustainable, Profitable Rabbit Farming Operation

Creating a sustainable, profitable rabbit farming operation takes a careful balance of best practices, meticulous record-keeping, and commitment to eco-friendly, long-term strategies. Backyard rabbit farming can be highly rewarding, with opportunities for regular income, sustainable food production, and minimal environmental impact. However, achieving this balance requires consistent effort in managing records and implementing sustainable practices.

1. Record-Keeping and Tracking Profits

Detailed record-keeping is essential to running a profitable rabbit farm. Keeping accurate records helps you make informed decisions, monitor the health of your rabbits, and manage finances effectively. **Here's how to approach it:**

Track Animal Health and Breeding Records: Maintain a health log for each rabbit, noting vaccinations, illnesses, and any special treatments. A breeding record, with details on lineage, mating dates, litter sizes, and growth rates, can help maximize productivity and improve genetic quality over time.

Monitor Feed and Supply Costs: Track the cost of feed, bedding, supplements, and other essential supplies. Knowing these expenses enables you to calculate the cost per rabbit and assess profitability accurately.

Labor and Time Investment: Record the time spent on daily tasks, such as feeding, cleaning, and healthcare. Over time, you can streamline these tasks to improve efficiency.

Sales and Revenue Tracking: Track the revenue from meat, pelts, or other products. Record customer feedback to ensure quality and explore potential pricing adjustments.

By analyzing these records regularly, you can identify profitable trends, make adjustments, and calculate the true costs and profits of your operation.

2. Sustainable Practices for Long-Term Success in Backyard Rabbit Farming

Adopting sustainable practices is crucial for long-term profitability and environmental health. Sustainability not only reduces costs but also minimizes your farm's ecological footprint. Here's how to incorporate sustainable practices:

Efficient Waste Management: Rabbit manure is a valuable fertilizer. Use a composting system to transform waste into rich compost for gardens, reducing waste and creating a valuable product for plant growth.

Natural and Locally-Sourced Feed: Where possible, use natural, locally-sourced feed to reduce transportation costs and environmental impact. Consider growing fodder crops, like alfalfa or clover, which can supplement the rabbits' diet and lower feed expenses.

Rotational Grazing Systems: If your setup allows, implement rotational grazing, which allows rabbits to forage naturally in small areas. This reduces feed costs and keeps the animals stimulated, helping maintain a healthy environment and happier rabbits.

Efficient Water Use: Use water-efficient systems, such as nipple waterers, to minimize waste. Regularly monitor and repair any leaks, ensuring water is used efficiently and responsibly.

Sustainable Breeding Practices: Implement controlled breeding to prevent overpopulation, focusing on quality over quantity. Select breeding pairs that exhibit healthy growth, good temperament, and disease resistance.

By combining rigorous record-keeping with eco-friendly practices, you can build a sustainable rabbit farming operation that is both profitable and responsible. This approach ensures that your farm remains productive, efficient, and aligned with environmental goals—paving the way for long-term success in backyard rabbit farming.